SOLVING THE MYSTERY IN HOW COMPUTERS CAME TO BE IN THE SIMPLEST LANGUAGE: THE SECRETS NO ONE HAS EVER TOLD YOU!

BY

NAWAS NAZIR

DEDICATION

Dedicated to anyone who wants to know how the computer really works but couldn't find anything satisfying.

HISTORICAL BACKGROUND AND EXPLANATION

1.1 HISTORICAL BACKGROUND AND EXPLANATION

The idea behind the computer hardware and software is always nothing more than arranging things in such a way that when so and so happens based on their behavior, then this and that occurs, appearing as if those things obey commands as we do! For example, imagine a zinc roof. When it gets heated by the sun, it makes a sound of expansion. This is as if someone commanded it to make sound whenever it is heated! Another clear example is the automatic door in which it appears as if someone commanded it that "whenever, you see someone trying to enter, you should open, yourself!" while in reality, what is happening is that some things are arranged in such a way that one generates voltage when temperature rises due to the presence of human body. Another one which is just a switch gets energized by this voltage and it activates a mechanical device that opens the door.

The processor is the computer itself. It is where things happen. Modern processors consists of mainly transistors which are mostly used as switches. Information or instructions are represented in the form of some switches being ON and others OFF such that, that way, they collectively cause something to happen due to some behaviour and properties.

THE BASIC INSIGHT

1.2 THE BASIC INSIGHT

People are saying that computers understand zero's and one's. What is meant by computer's understanding even? What are these zero's and one's? Are they the numbers we know? Nope! Only you as a human being. know that. In reality, these zeros and ones are nothing but VOLTAGES. Some level of voltage can cause the transistor switch to get turned on. This is what we call a "1" while the level of voltage that cannot turn the transistor switch is what is termed as a "0" since it is nothing as it can't turn on a switch. Note that all these switches represent instructions or commands or data as they put control on how something is to be done by the other components of the computer e.g. how they interact with the screen (whose function is to display) in order to display the object desired. As an example, if one press the letter "A", this is what happens;

The ASCII code for letter A is 01000001. This means that the letter A on the keyboard is connected to 8 transistors through eight lines; only a single voltage value (1 or 0) can follow a line. Thus, when you press the capital letter A on the keyboard, the computer's power supply is used to provide two high voltages (1's) and six low voltages (0's) in the order above i.e first line 0, second line 1,.....(according to the A=01000001). These voltages cause current to flow to switch ON two transistors and leave untouched, the others (since it is zeros i.e.

'nothings' are sent to them).

This set of transistors, this way, cause some components arranged in some ways to show the letter "A" on the screen.

WHAT IS SOFTWARE AND WHY SOFTWARE?

1.3 WHAT IS SOFTWARE AND WHY SOFTWARE?

In the early computers, the switches or things i.e. components are arranged such that the whole computer behaves in a certain way making it possible to perform a particular task. This means that whenever you want to perform a different task, you must change how things are arranged and sometimes, you must have to substitute some components with new ones. This is costly and not easy.

As a result of this, the idea of software came into being. It was possible with the advent of programmable devices. These are nothing but devices whose states can be changed (using voltages) to suit a particular purpose. As any software is nothing but basically, a collection of zeros and ones which as we mentioned earlier are nothing more than voltages (stored in computer memory), then whenever we have software running on a programmable device or loaded into a programmable device, it changes the state of the device, rendering it ready for executing a job specified by the software i.e. a job which the software is meant for. Thus, whenever we want the computer to do a different task, the current software in the working memory (RAM), is taken to a secondary storage e.g. the hard drive and is replaced with another software we want. This way, with a single hardware, many tasks can be executed without the need of

changing the components arrangement, adding or removing some

components or substituting some components with others unless if the

present components don't have the required properties.

WHAT IS COMPILER AND WHY COMPILER?

1.4 WHAT IS COMPILER AND WHY COMPILER?

Compiler is nothing but a software and we explained why we need software. Compiler is a software that enables converting what we write in a so called "programming language " into machine language in which we said software is nothing but collection of zeros and ones i.e. voltages.

But how does this conversion take place? How do we tell the compiler that if we write so and so in this programming language, this is what it should do? We have what is known as the assembler. The assembler is a software that converts a program written in an assembly language into machine codes. Assembly language is a language which depends on the architecture of the given hardware. Hardware engineers arranged things in a computer such that it understands a desired language i.e. assembly language (called assembly language because it is a language defined by the arrangement of components of the computer i.e. defined right from the stage of assembling the components). As an example, a common and familiar code in assembly languages is the "MOV A, B" which means to move the contents of register (memory) A to register B. How it is done is this way:

The components (transistors and all other necessary things) are arranged in such a way that when M is typed, some set of transistors become ON and some OFF. Similar goes for the O, V and all other parts of the code. This combination based on the design will activate all components required in the transfer of the contents of register A into B through what they call bus i.e. path.

Coming back to the compiler, it depends on the assembler to use the hardware. The first compiler was written in assembly language in which we simply choose some words we want and write that whenever they are encountered by the software (the compiler) , they mean so and so i.e. this and that should happen and thus, arriving at a new computer language called the high level language like the C++ , Java and what have you.

From then, everything become simple as it is just the matter of building upon. For instance, we can have a compiler (i.e. new language) developed using another language e.g. writing a Java compiler in C.

QUESTION: What is the essence of the compiler and high level language since we can develop a software in assembly language with an assembler and moreover, the first compiler was written in assembly language and assembly language is closest to the machine language (zeros and ones) and it is from the hardware manufacturers who know the computer the best?

The answer is simple. Assembly language is far from human language making it inconvenient to retain and to do a simple task in assembly language, we have to write many lines of codes and to write in assembly language we need to know the hardware and how the components interact with each other. With high level languages in which compilers are used all these shortcomings are overcomed!

WHAT IS COMPILATION AND HOW DOES IT TAKE PLACE?

1.4.1 WHAT IS COMPILATION AND HOW DOES IT TAKE PLACE?

Whenever we want to write a program or software that should do something e.g. a software that should be adding two numbers, then it means we want to instruct the computer and so, we must do that in a language the computer understands i.e. in zeros and ones(machine language) or something based on zeros and ones i.e. based on the arrangement of components i.e. assembly language or based on the assembly language i.e. the high level language.

To instruct the computer to do something in a given high level language, we write the instructions in a compiler for that language. The function of the compiler is reading and translating whatever we have written in the appropriate high level language into assembly language which is then converted to the zeros and ones through a process called compilation (Remember that we explained how a compiler works i.e. how it compiles things- SEE THE "WHY COMPILER AND HOW IT WORKS"). It is this compilation product we call software which we install and use. The compilation product which is nothing but zeros and ones can be stored in memory i.e. each memory cell will hold a single 1 or 0.

The memory cell is nothing but a capacitor or a transistor. And so, to hold a zero, the capacitor will have no any charge to store while the transistor will have a voltage that keeps it OFF. On the other hand, to store a 1, the capacitor in the respective cell would have charge to store while the transistor would get the voltage that would keep it ON. This way we store the software (zeros and ones) in the memory cells. To run the program, on your computer what happens is that the states of the transistors or capacitors in the memory cells are copied into the processor's transistors, thus setting everything for things desired to happen, happen.

WHAT IS INTERPRETER?

1.5 WHAT IS INTERPRETER?

Interpreter is just like a compiler only that it translates a program line by line. It is only after a line of code in the program is translated i.e. converted to zeros and ones and the task specified in the line is executed before another line is taken. Unlike a compiler in which all of the lines in a program are translated and converted into zeros and ones before execution starts.

WHAT IS OPERATING SYSTEM AND HOW DOES IT WORK?

1.6 **WHAT IS OPERATING SYSTEM AND HOW DOES IT WORK?**

Operating system is nothing but a software and is developed using a programming language e.g. the C language just as all other softwares are. The only special thing about it, is that it is a software written in such a way that it is given the control of all computer resources, such that no any software can use anything unless it gives permission for that. And all these capabilities are no magic, as it is just the matter of instructing the computer through a programming language which we have already discussed.

FOR QUESTIONS, INQUIRIES OR COMMENTS CONTACT THE AUTHOR THROUGH;

E-mail: nawasnaziru@gmail.com

Website: imindware.blogspot.com

Phone: +2348137890313

www.ingramcontent.com/pod-product-compliance
Lightning Source LLC
Chambersburg PA
CBHW061100050326
40690CB00012B/2686